bajc

EDGE BOOKS

ORIGAMI
Explosion

Scorpions, Whales, Boxes, and More!

by Christopher Harbo

CAPSTONE PRESS
a capstone imprint

Edge Books are published by Capstone Press,
1710 Roe Crest Drive, North Mankato, Minnesota 56003
www.capstonepub.com

Library of Congress Cataloging-in-Publication Data
Harbo, Christopher L., author.
  Origami explosion : scorpions, whales, boxes, and more! / by Christopher Harbo.
    pages cm.—(Edge books. Origami paperpalooza)
  Summary: "Provides instructions and photo-illustrated step diagrams for folding a variety of traditional and original origami models"—Provided by publisher.
  Audience: Ages 8-14.
  Audience: Grades 4 to 6.
  Includes bibliographical references.
  ISBN 978-1-4914-2023-2 (library binding)
  ISBN 978-1-4914-2194-9 (eBook PDF)
1. Origami—Juvenile literature. 2. Handicraft—Juvenile literature. I. Title.
  TT872.5.H374 2015
  736.982—dc23   2014027874

Editorial Credits
Sarah Bennett, designer; Kathy McColley, layout artist; Katy LaVigne, production specialist; Marcy Morin, scheduler

Photo Credits
All photographs done by Capstone Studio: Karon Dubke

Design Elements: Shutterstock: naihei

The author thanks Ingrid Harbo for illustrating the faces on the animal finger puppets shown on page 8.

Printed in Canada.
102014   008478FRS15

Table of Contents

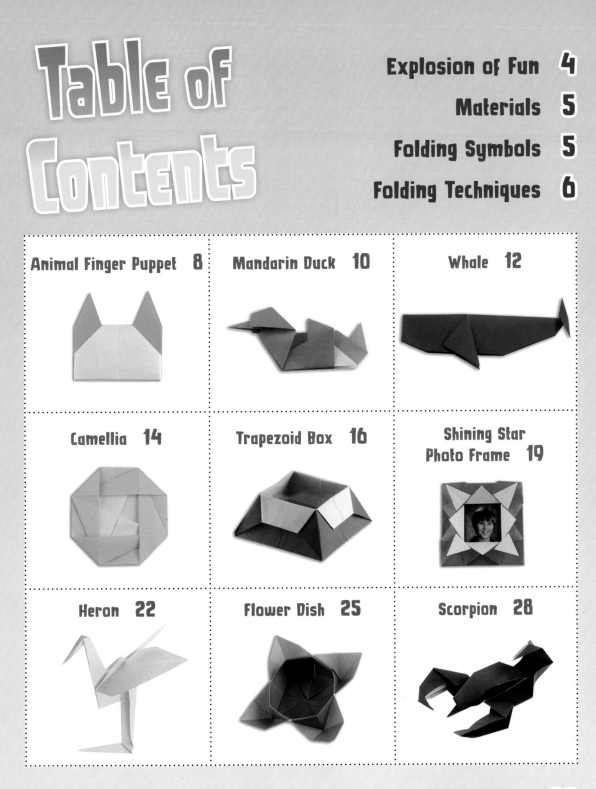

Explosion of Fun

Brace yourself! You're about to have a blast with the Japanese art of paper folding. This collection of traditional and original origami models is guaranteed to amaze. Showcase a friend's picture in a folded photo frame that bursts with color. Fold a paper scorpion complete with pincers and a sharp stinger. Create clever boxes to stash your favorite treasures. From herons to flower dishes to finger puppets, an amazing variety of paper projects is at your fingertips. What are you waiting for? Stretch your fingers and let's start folding. An origami explosion awaits!

Materials

Origami is an affordable hobby because it doesn't require many materials to get started. In fact, you'll only need a square sheet of paper for most of the models in this book. A few models may require some extra materials, but you can easily find most of these items around the house:

Paper: While you can fold with just about any paper, authentic origami paper often works best. It is perfectly square, easy to fold, and has a crispness that holds its creases well. You'll find packets of origami paper with many fun colors, patterns, and sizes at most craft stores.

Scissors: Sometimes a model needs a snip here or there to pull off a key detail. You won't need it often, but keep a pair of scissors handy.

Ruler: Some models use measurements to complete. A ruler will help you measure.

Paper Trimmer: A good quality paper trimmer will come in handy when you want to cut paper to a custom size. Rotary blade paper trimmers are a good choice for precise, clean cutting. A variety of paper trimmers can be found at any craft store.

Pencil: Use a pencil when you need to mark a spot with the ruler.

Craft Supplies: Markers and other craft supplies will help you decorate your finished models.

Folding Symbols

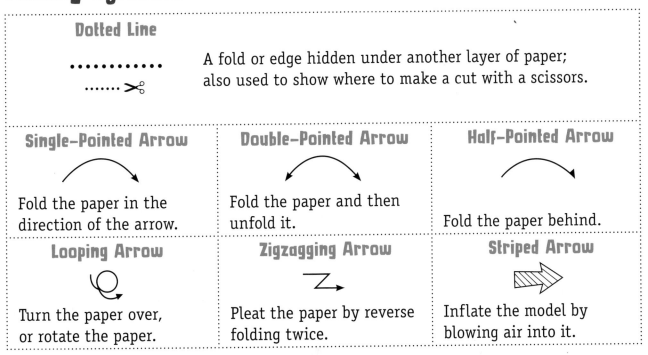

Dotted Line	
●●●●●●●●●●● ●●●●●✂	A fold or edge hidden under another layer of paper; also used to show where to make a cut with a scissors.

Single-Pointed Arrow	Double-Pointed Arrow	Half-Pointed Arrow
Fold the paper in the direction of the arrow.	Fold the paper and then unfold it.	Fold the paper behind.
Looping Arrow	**Zigzagging Arrow**	**Striped Arrow**
Turn the paper over, or rotate the paper.	Pleat the paper by reverse folding twice.	Inflate the model by blowing air into it.

Folding Techniques

Folding paper is easier when you understand basic origami folding terms and techniques. Practice the folds below before trying the models in this book. Bookmark these pages so you can refer back to them if you get stuck on a tricky step.

Valley folds are represented by a dashed line. One side of the paper is folded against the other like a book.

Mountain folds are represented by a dashed and dotted line. The paper is folded sharply behind the model.

Squash folds are formed by lifting one edge of a pocket. The pocket gets folded again so the spine gets flattened. The existing fold lines become new edges.

Inside reverse folds are made by opening a pocket slightly. Then you fold the model inside itself along the fold lines or existing creases.

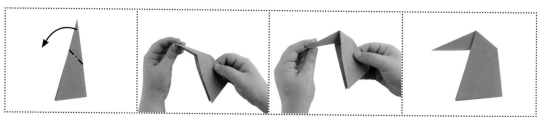

Outside reverse folds are made by opening a pocket slightly. Then you fold the model outside itself along the fold lines or existing creases.

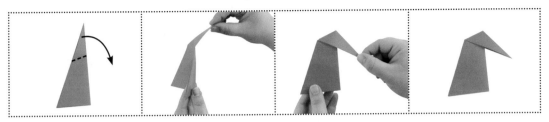

Rabbit ear folds are formed by bringing two edges of a point together using existing fold lines. The new point is folded to one side.

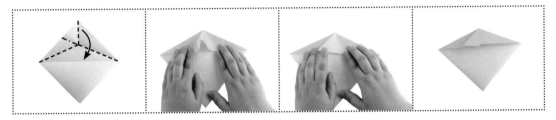

Petal folds are made by pulling a point upward and allowing its sides to come together as the paper flattens.

Pleat folds are made by using both a mountain fold and a valley fold.

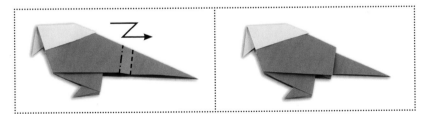

Mark folds are light folds used to make reference creases for a later step. Ideally a mark fold will not be seen in the finished model.

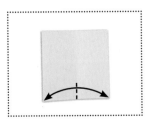

Animal Finger Puppet ◆ Traditional

Tap into your imagination with this simple animal finger puppet. Depending on how you fold the ears, it can look like a cat, a dog, or even a pig.

Tip: Complete your finger puppet by drawing a face on the front of the model.

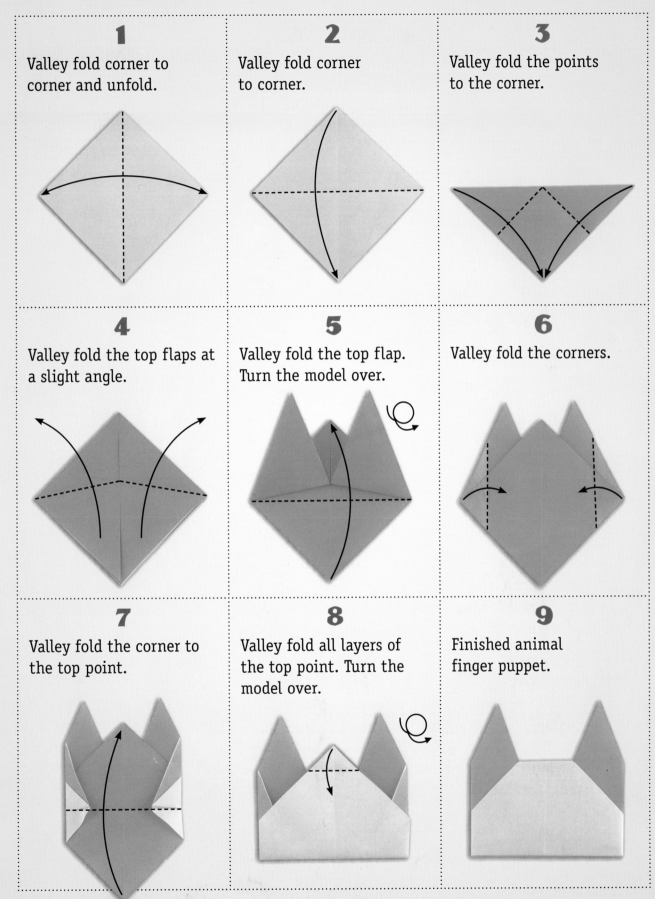

1
Valley fold corner to corner and unfold.

2
Valley fold corner to corner.

3
Valley fold the points to the corner.

4
Valley fold the top flaps at a slight angle.

5
Valley fold the top flap. Turn the model over.

6
Valley fold the corners.

7
Valley fold the corner to the top point.

8
Valley fold all layers of the top point. Turn the model over.

9
Finished animal finger puppet.

Mandarin Duck ◆ Traditional

The male mandarin duck is known for the "sail" feathers that stick up from his back. This model uses that feature to create a truly unique origami duck.

1
Valley fold corner to corner and unfold.

2
Valley fold the edges to the center. Turn the model over.

3
Valley fold the right corner about ¾ of the way to the left point.

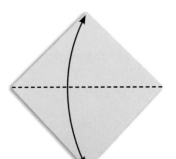
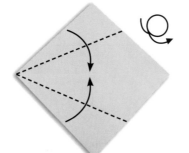

4

Valley fold the top flap along the vertical edge.

5

Mountain fold the model in half.

6

Valley fold the top layer so the dot meets the top edge. Repeat behind.

7

Outside reverse fold so the dot meets the top edge.

8

Outside reverse fold the point to make the head.

9

Pleat fold the head to make the beak.

10

Pleat fold the point to make a tail.

11

Finished mandarin duck.

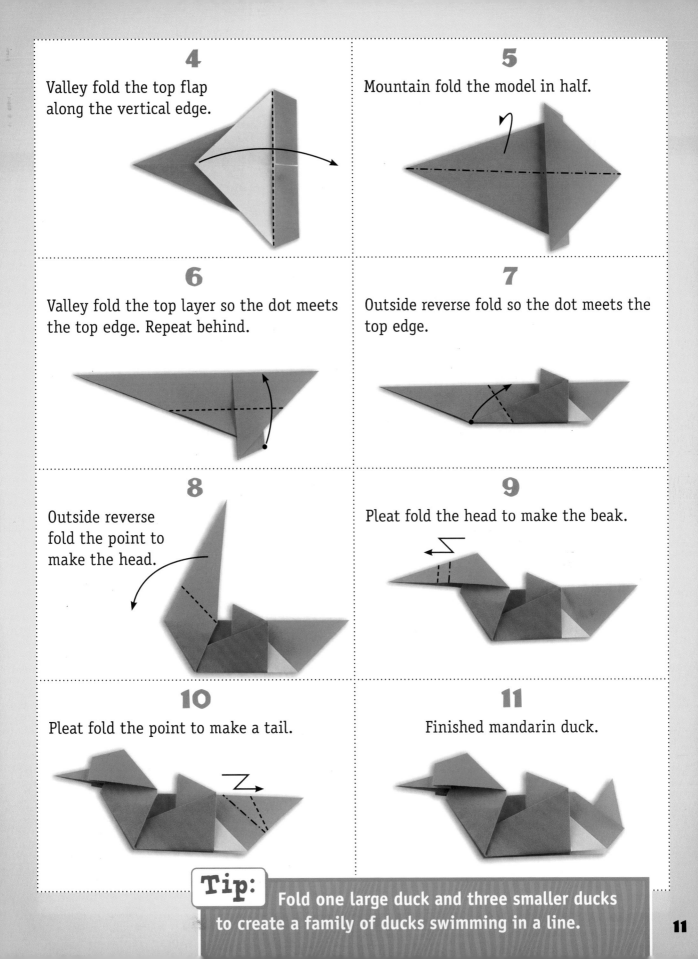

Tip: Fold one large duck and three smaller ducks to create a family of ducks swimming in a line.

Whale ◆ Traditional

Thar she blows! Gray and blue whales are giants of the sea. Make your paper versions large or small in any color you like.

1

Valley fold corner to corner in both directions and unfold.

2

Valley fold the edges to the center and unfold.

3

Valley fold the edges to the center and unfold.

4

Rabbit ear fold on the existing creases.

5

Turn the model over.

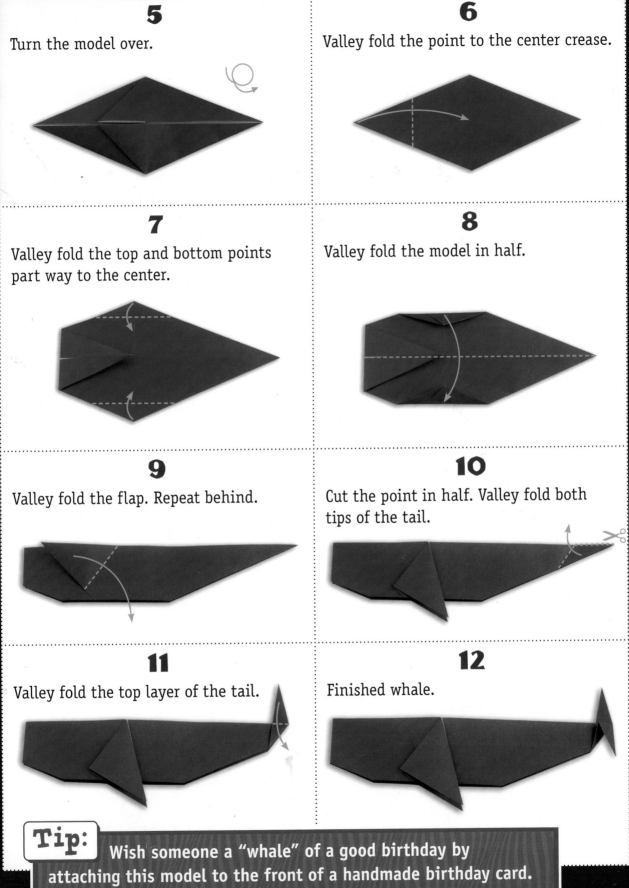

6

Valley fold the point to the center crease.

7

Valley fold the top and bottom points part way to the center.

8

Valley fold the model in half.

9

Valley fold the flap. Repeat behind.

10

Cut the point in half. Valley fold both tips of the tail.

11

Valley fold the top layer of the tail.

12

Finished whale.

Tip: Wish someone a "whale" of a good birthday by attaching this model to the front of a handmade birthday card.

Camellia ◆ Traditional

Camellias are flowering trees and shrubs originally from southern and eastern Asia. Today more than 3,000 types of camellias bloom around the world.

1

Valley fold corner to corner in both directions and unfold.

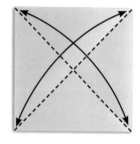

2

Valley fold the edge to the center.

Tip: Create the swirling petals seen in real camellias by layering three models of different sizes.

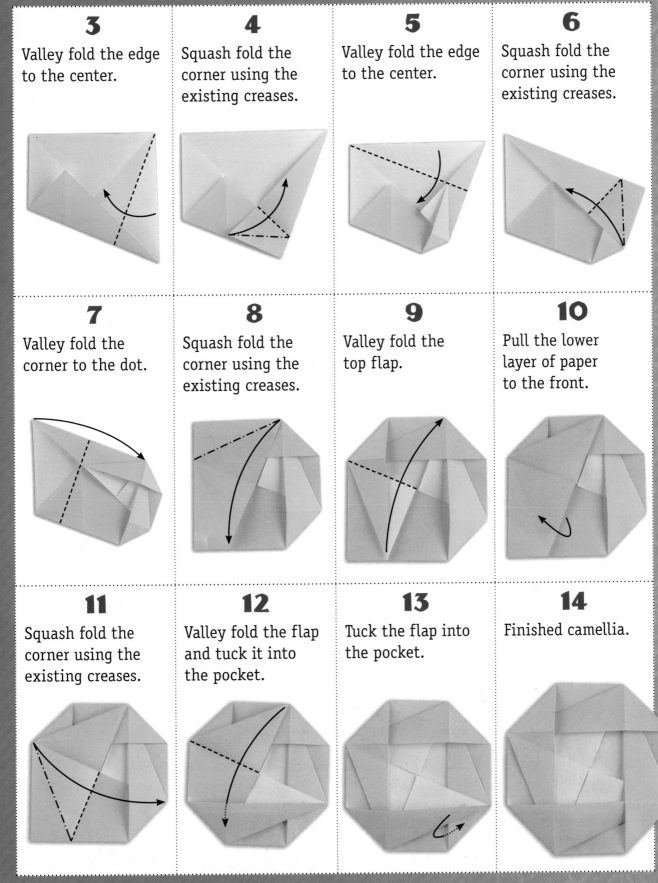

3
Valley fold the edge to the center.

4
Squash fold the corner using the existing creases.

5
Valley fold the edge to the center.

6
Squash fold the corner using the existing creases.

7
Valley fold the corner to the dot.

8
Squash fold the corner using the existing creases.

9
Valley fold the top flap.

10
Pull the lower layer of paper to the front.

11
Squash fold the corner using the existing creases.

12
Valley fold the flap and tuck it into the pocket.

13
Tuck the flap into the pocket.

14
Finished camellia.

Trapezoid Box ◆ Traditional

The trapezoid box gains strength from its inward slanting sides. Fill it up! You'll be surprised by how much stuff this nifty box can hold.

Tip: Write someone's name on the side of the box. Then fill the box with crackers or candy and use it to mark a spot at the dinner table.

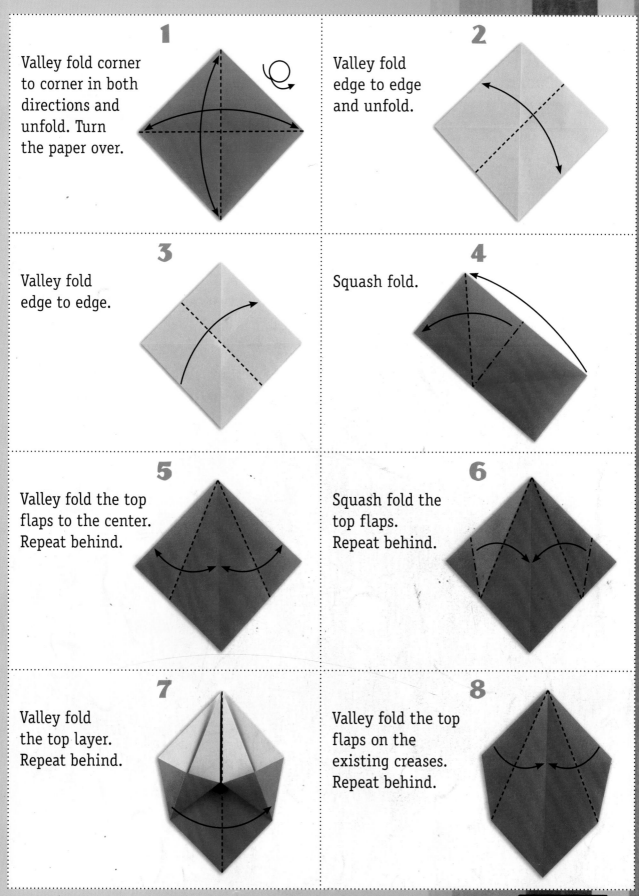

1 Valley fold corner to corner in both directions and unfold. Turn the paper over.

2 Valley fold edge to edge and unfold.

3 Valley fold edge to edge.

4 Squash fold.

5 Valley fold the top flaps to the center. Repeat behind.

6 Squash fold the top flaps. Repeat behind.

7 Valley fold the top layer. Repeat behind.

8 Valley fold the top flaps on the existing creases. Repeat behind.

9

Valley fold the bottom corner and unfold.

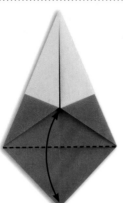

10

Valley fold the top flap two times and tuck the extra paper into the pocket. Repeat behind.

11

Valley fold the top layer. Repeat behind.

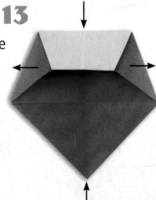

12

Repeat step 10 on the remaining two sides.

13

Open the top of the model and gently pull out the sides. At the same time, push up on the bottom point to form the box.

14

Finished trapezoid box.

Shining Star Photo Frame ◆

Traditional model adapted by Christopher Harbo

Showcase your wallet-sized photos with stunning photo frames. For the perfect size, fold the model with a 6-inch (15-centimeter) square of paper.

 Tip: Glue a small magnet to the back of your photo frame to stick it inside a school locker.

1

Valley fold edge to edge and unfold.

2

Valley fold the edges to the center.

3

Valley fold edge to edge and unfold.

4

Valley fold the edges to the center and unfold.

5

Valley fold the edge to the creases made in step 4 and unfold.

6

Squash fold on the existing creases.

7

Valley fold the inside edges of each flap to the center.

8

Squash fold all four points.

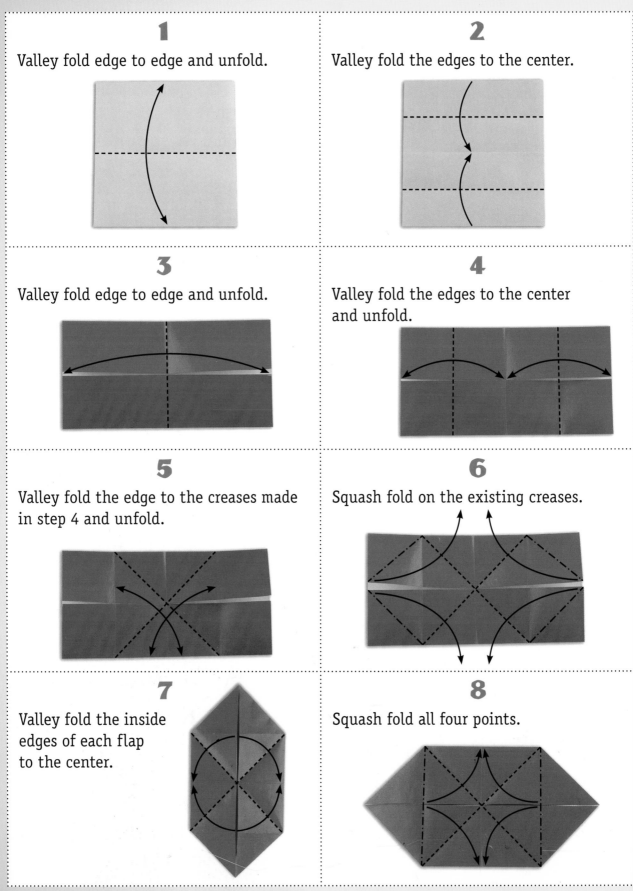

9

Valley fold the edges of each of the four squares to their center creases.

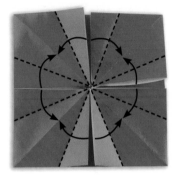

10

Squash fold all of the triangles.

11

Valley fold all four points.

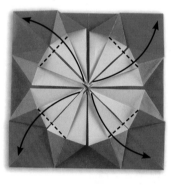

12

Valley fold all four points.

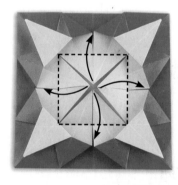

13

Place a wallet-size photo inside the frame.

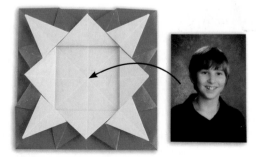

14

Finished shining star photo frame.

Heron ◆ Traditional

Herons stand motionless on their long legs to hunt for fish in shallow water. Once you've folded your paper heron, see if it will stand on its own.

1

Valley fold corner to corner in both directions and unfold. Turn the paper over.

2

Valley fold edge to edge and unfold.

3

Valley fold edge to edge.

4

Squash fold.

5

Valley fold the top flaps to the center and unfold. Repeat behind.

6

Inside reverse fold the top flaps. Repeat behind.

7

Valley fold the top flap. Repeat behind.

8

Valley fold the top flaps to the center. Repeat behind.

9

Inside reverse fold the left point upward.

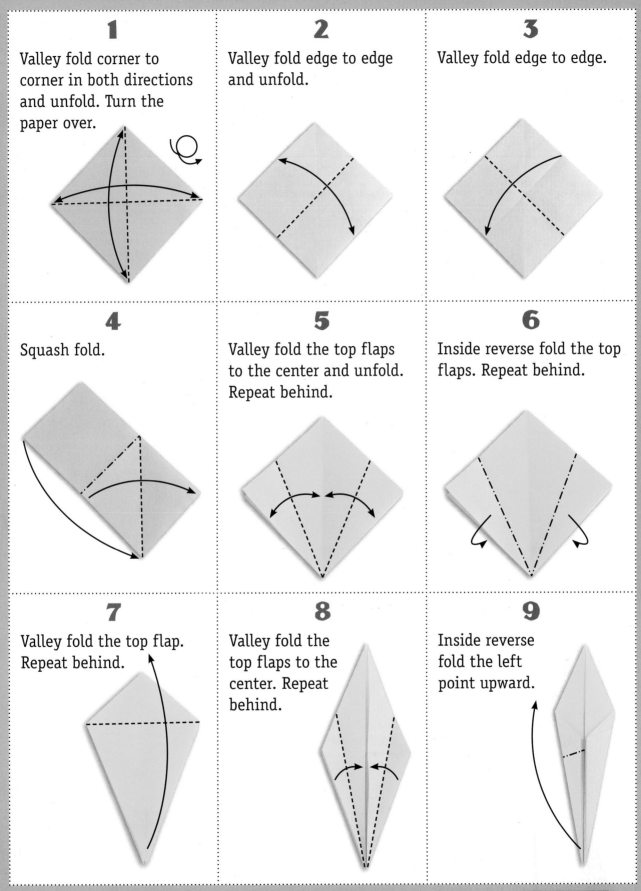

Continued ➡

10

Inside reverse fold the point to form the head.

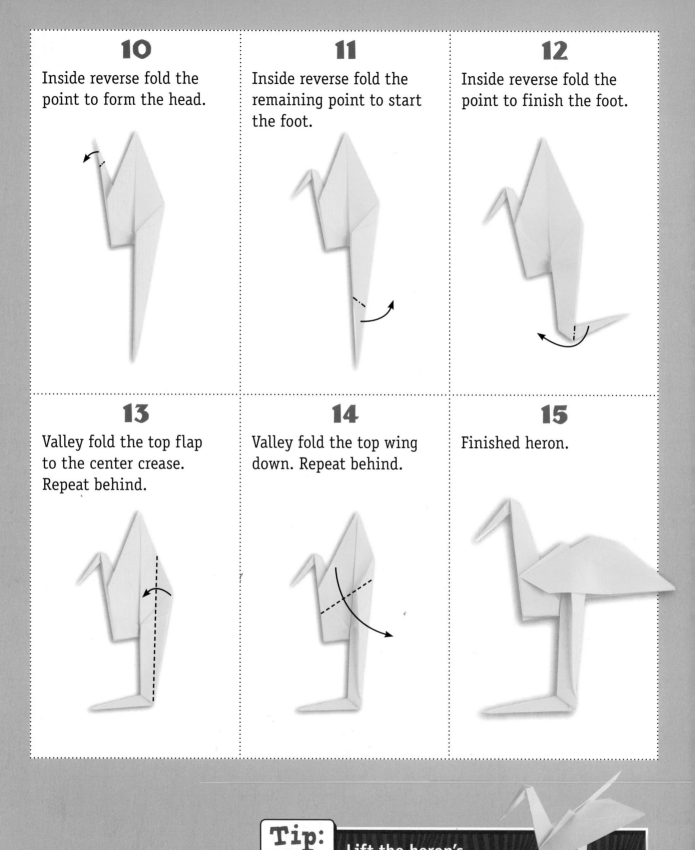

11

Inside reverse fold the remaining point to start the foot.

12

Inside reverse fold the point to finish the foot.

13

Valley fold the top flap to the center crease. Repeat behind.

14

Valley fold the top wing down. Repeat behind.

15

Finished heron.

Tip: Lift the heron's wings up halfway to give the model a dynamic 3-D look.

Flower Dish ◆ Traditional

The flower dish combines function and beauty. Its strong sides can handle heavy loads while looking pretty at the same time.

Tip: Use the flower dish's petals to hold items too. For instance, a single jellybean in each petal would complement a pile of chocolates in the center of the dish.

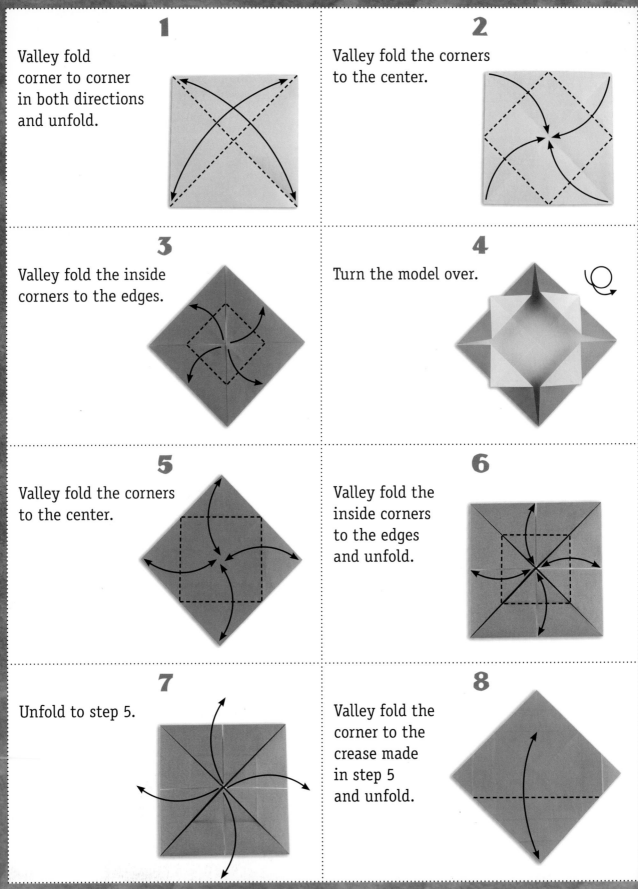

1

Valley fold corner to corner in both directions and unfold.

2

Valley fold the corners to the center.

3

Valley fold the inside corners to the edges.

4

Turn the model over.

5

Valley fold the corners to the center.

6

Valley fold the inside corners to the edges and unfold.

7

Unfold to step 5.

8

Valley fold the corner to the crease made in step 5 and unfold.

9

Repeat step 8 on the other three corners.

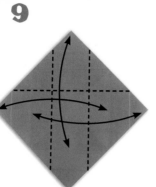

10

Valley fold two corners to the center.

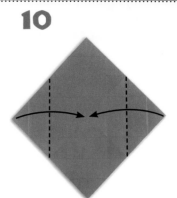

11

Valley fold the right edge and top halfway. Allow the loose flap on the corner to release.

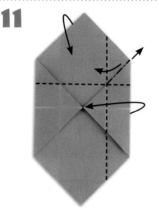

12

Valley fold the left edge halfway. Allow the loose flap on the corner to release.

13

Valley fold the point into the box. The top of the point will mountain fold into the bottom of the box.

14

Repeat step 13 on the bottom of the model.

15

Shape the sides of the dish to make it round.

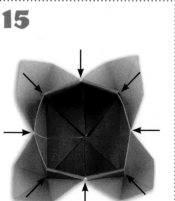

16

Finished flower dish.

Scorpion ◆ by Christopher Harbo

Two pincers and a curved tail are the trademarks of the scorpion. Luckily, you can fold this specimen without the fear of getting stung.

1

Valley fold corner to corner in both directions and unfold. Turn the paper over.

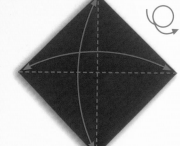

2

Valley fold edge to edge and unfold.

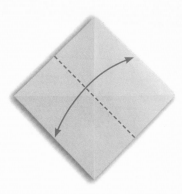

3

Valley fold edge to edge.

4

Squash fold.

5

Valley fold the top flaps to the center and unfold. Repeat behind.

6

Inside reverse fold the top flaps. Repeat behind.

7

Valley fold the top flap. Repeat behind.

8

Valley fold the top flaps to the center. Repeat behind.

9

Valley fold the points upward and unfold.

10
Inside reverse fold on the creases made in step 9.

11
Inside reverse fold the points downward.

12
Outside reverse fold the points to make claws.

13
Valley fold the top point as far as it will go.

14
Turn the model over.

15
Valley fold the point.

16
Valley fold the point.

17
Valley fold the top point as far as it will go.

18
Valley fold the edges to the center and unfold.

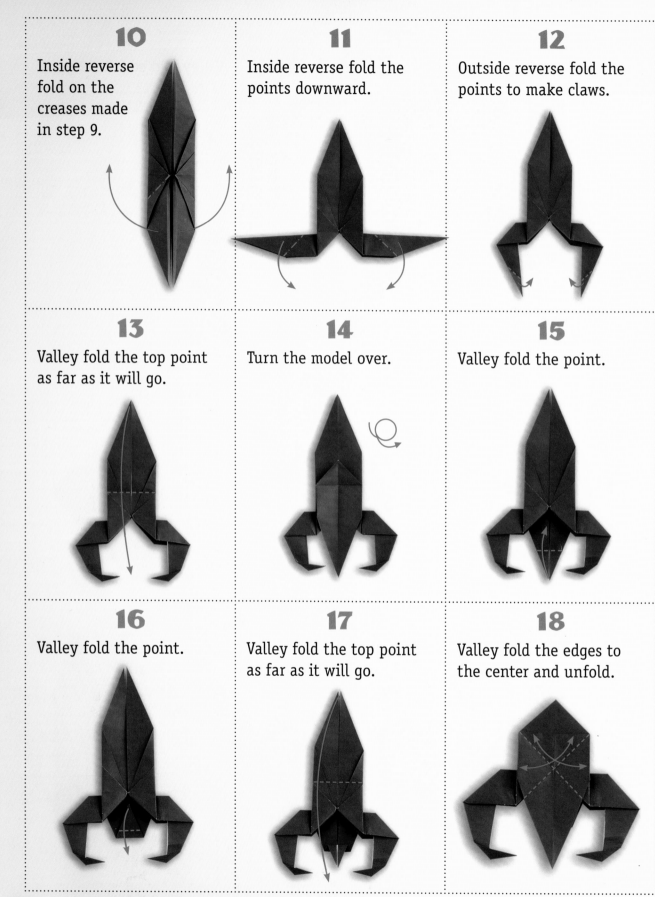

19

Unfold the point. Turn the model over.

20

Swing the tail up around the triangle at the top of the body.

21

Pinch the tail to allow it to stand straight up.

22

Inside reverse fold the tail.

23

Outside reverse fold the tip of the tail.

24

Valley fold the entire model in half and unfold slightly.

25

Finished scorpion.

Tip: Add an extra inside reverse fold to the tip of the stinger to make your scorpion's tail extra curly.

Read More

Bolitho, Mark. *Fold Your Own Origami Navy*. Origami Army.
New York: PowerKids Press, 2014.

Miles, Lisa. *Origami Wild Animals*. Amazing Origami.
New York: Gareth Stevens Publishing, 2014.

Owen, Ruth. *Ocean Animals*. Origami Safari. New York:
Windmill Books, 2015.

Internet Sites

FactHound offers a safe, fun way to find Internet sites related to this book. All of the sites on FactHound have been researched by our staff.

Here's all you do:
Visit *www.facthound.com*
Type in this code: 9781491420232

 Check out projects, games and lots more at
www.capstonekids.com

About the Author

Christopher Harbo has a passion for origami. He began folding paper 10 years ago when he tried making a simple model for his nephews. With that first successful creation, he quickly became hooked on the art form. He ran to his local library and checked out every origami book he could find to increase his folding skills. Today he continues to develop his origami skills and loves the thrill of folding new creations. In addition to traditional origami and its many uses, he also enjoys folding paper airplanes and modular origami. When he's not folding paper, Christopher spends his free time reading Japanese manga and watching movies.